THIS BOOK BELONGS TO

_____

START DATE

_____

SHE READS TRUTH

@SHEREADSTRUTH

Download the
She Reads Truth app,
available for iOS
and Android

Subscribe to the
She Reads Truth podcast

SHEREADSTRUTH.COM

EXECUTIVE

FOUNDER/CHIEF EXECUTIVE OFFICER
Raechel Myers

CO-FOUNDER/CHIEF CONTENT OFFICER
Amanda Bible Williams

CHIEF OPERATING OFFICER
Ryan Myers

EXECUTIVE ASSISTANT
Sarah Andereck

EDITORIAL

EDITORIAL DIRECTOR
Jessica Lamb

MANAGING EDITOR
Beth Joseph

CONTENT EDITOR
Kara Gause

ASSOCIATE EDITORS
Bailey Gillespie
Tameshia Williams

EDITORIAL ASSISTANT
Hannah Little

EDITORIAL INTERN
Bailey Shoemaker

MARKETING

MARKETING MANAGER
Katie Matuska Pierce

SOCIAL MEDIA STRATEGIST
Taylor Krupp

COMMUNITY SUPPORT SPECIALIST
Margot Williams

CREATIVE

CREATIVE DIRECTOR
Jeremy Mitchell

LEAD DESIGNER
Kelsea Allen

DESIGNERS
Abbey Benson
Davis Camp DeLisi
Annie Glover

JUNIOR DESIGNER
Lauren Haag

LOGISTICS & SHIPPING

LOGISTICS MANAGER
Lauren Gloyne

CUSTOMER SUPPORT MANAGER
Kara Hewett

PROJECT ASSISTANT
Mary Beth Montgomery

CUSTOMER SUPPORT SPECIALISTS
Elise Matson
Katy McKnight

FULFILLMENT LEAD
Abigail Achord

FULFILLMENT SPECIALISTS
Cait Baggerman
Noe Sanchez

SUBSCRIPTION INQUIRIES
orders@shereadstruth.com

CONTRIBUTOR

PHOTOGRAPHY
Jessica Steddom (41, 65)

SHE READS TRUTH™

© 2021 by She Reads Truth, LLC

All rights reserved.

All photography used by permission.

ISBN 978-1-952670-33-6

1 2 3 4 5 6 7 8 9 10

Unless otherwise noted, Scripture is taken from the Christian Standard Bible®. Copyright © 2020 by Holman Bible Publishers. Used by permission. Christian Standard Bible® and CSB® are federally registered trademarks of Holman Bible Publishers.

Scripture quotations marked NIV are taken from the Holy Bible, New International Version®, NIV®. Copyright © 1973, 1978, 1984, 2011 by Biblica, Inc.™ Used by permission of Zondervan. All rights reserved worldwide. www.zondervan.com. The "NIV" and "New International Version" are trademarks registered in the United States Patent and Trademark Office by Biblica, Inc.™

Verses omitted in the CSB are also omitted in this book.

Research support provided by Logos Bible Software™. Learn more at logos.com.

This book was printed offset in Nashville, Tennessee, on 70# Lynx Opaque. Cover is 100# Cougar Opaque with a soft touch lamination.

ONE ANOTHER

A BIBLICAL STUDY OF CHRISTIAN COMMUNITY

SHE READS TRUTH

Jesus brings each one of us mismatched pieces into something meticulously crafted and beautiful: His people, the body of Christ.

Jessica
Jessica Lamb
EDITORIAL DIRECTOR

One evening in high school, I decided to make a quilt. So with mediocre sewing skills, my preconceived notions of the quilting process, and no further research, I got to work. Concert t-shirts, jeans, scraps of silk, an old volleyball jersey—I cut every spare piece of fabric I could find into messy, uneven squares. After arranging them into a haphazard pattern, I started sewing. The process did not go smoothly. I knew nothing of pre-washing fabrics, ironing seams, or how different materials would work alongside one another. But after months of tears and fighting with my sewing machine, I wrangled the material into something resembling a quilt top that my grandmother mercifully completed with a backing.

The finished product has no business existing. It's not much to look at, and it certainly fails to meet even the most generous standard for visual appeal. But to this day, I keep it in a basket next to my couch, carefully folded alongside the more meticulously crafted quilts I've inherited. It's precious to me because, in spite of its flaws and shortcomings, it's my own.

My mind kept returning to my quilt as our team worked on this reading plan about life in Christian community. I don't think I'm alone in feeling like life with other believers is often easier read about than lived. The family of God is messy. We're a disparate group of individuals from every imaginable nation, ethnicity, family circumstance, and political affiliation. Each one of us has a story, and we bring our own history of wounds and wounding to the family table.

Thankfully, this isn't new or surprising to God. From the first disciples and the early Church to our current cultural moment, the body of Christ has always been made up of believers who have no real reason for living in community together outside of the one reason that changes everything. Jesus brings each one of us mismatched pieces into something meticulously crafted and beautiful: His people, the body of Christ.

Over the next two weeks, we'll read a series of "one another" commands that describe the radical ways we're called to love our brothers and sisters in Christ because of who we are in Him. (Read more about these commands on page 12!) We'll also reflect on how knowing Jesus equips us to live differently in all relationships (see "How Should I Relate To...?" on page 52) and discover how our relationships with one another reflect Christ's transforming love.

I needed this reading plan, this reminder that learning to live well together is a good and worthwhile mission, even (or especially) when it isn't easy. No matter where this Study Book finds you, whether in a season of flourishing community or one of struggle and searching, my prayer is that you will be both challenged and encouraged through God's Word.

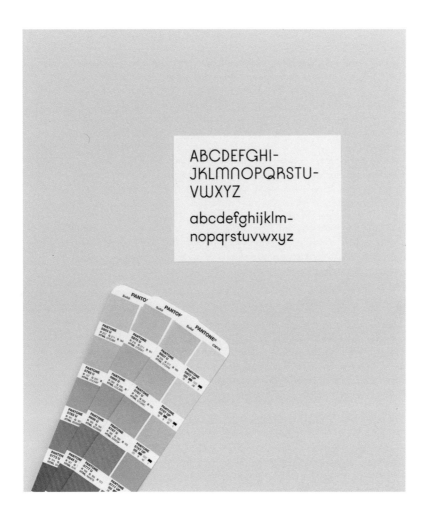

At She Reads Truth, we believe in pairing the inherently beautiful Word of God with the aesthetic beauty it deserves. Each of our resources is thoughtfully and artfully designed to highlight the beauty, goodness, and truth of Scripture in a way that reflects the themes of each curated reading plan.

This Study Book features photographs of people interacting in a variety of settings and relationships. These images are a celebration of community and point to the theme of Christian relationships explored in this plan.

HOW TO USE THIS BOOK

She Reads Truth is a community of women dedicated to reading the Word of God every day. The Bible is living and active, and we confidently hold it higher than anything we can do or say.

READ & REFLECT

This **One Another** Study Book focuses primarily on Scripture, with bonus resources to facilitate deeper engagement with God's Word.

SCRIPTURE READING

Designed for a Monday start, this Study Book presents daily readings on how we can live as part of a healthy gospel community in Christ.

DAILY REFLECTION

Each weekday features repeated questions for personal reflection.

COMMUNITY & CONVERSATION

Join women from Boise to Bermuda as they read with you!

 SHE READS TRUTH APP

Devotionals corresponding to each daily reading can be found in the **One Another** reading plan on the She Reads Truth app. You can also participate in community discussions, download free lock screens for Weekly Truth memorization, and more.

GRACE DAY

Use Saturdays to catch up on your reading, pray, and rest in the presence of the Lord.

WEEKLY TRUTH

Sundays are set aside for Scripture memorization.

EXTRAS

This book features additional tools to help you gain a deeper understanding of the text.

Find a complete list of extras on page 11.

 SHEREADSTRUTH.COM

All of our reading plans and devotionals are also available at SheReadsTruth.com. Invite your family, friends, and neighbors to read along with you!

 SHE READS TRUTH PODCAST

Join our She Reads Truth founders and their guests each Monday as they open their Bibles and talk about the beauty, goodness, and truth they find there. Each podcast episode corresponds to the current community reading plan. Subscribe on your favorite podcast app so you don't miss a conversation about the **One Another** reading plan and more.

Week One

Week Two

Extras

Introduction

What do we mean by "one another"?

Allélón (a–lay'–lone) is a single Greek word that is translated as two words: one another. This word refers to a reciprocal relationship between groups or entities where both parties are contributing. Often in the New Testament, it is used when people are talking together, but it is also used in several commands.

What are the "one another" commands?

The New Testament offers a series of "one another" commands using *allélón*. These commands are both positive (things we ought to do) and negative (things we shouldn't do), and speak to qualities that should define the Church, such as love, unity, service, correction, humility, and encouragement.

We've bolded each time allélón *or a related Greek word is translated "one another" in your daily Scripture reading.*

Who do these commands apply to?

Each of these New Testament commands speaks to how we should live as part of a healthy gospel community in Jesus. They are both aspirational and practical—a picture of the ideal, as well as commands we are called to pursue even as we and our brothers and sisters in Christ fall short.

If you are a follower of Jesus, these commands are directed to you. Though the Bible has a lot to say about how we should treat creation and others more generally (see "How Should I Relate To…?" on page 52 for more), the "one another" commands are specific to how those who have been made a new family through faith in Jesus are meant to behave toward other believers.

Are these the only verses that speak about Christian community?

No! Other verses in Scripture, some of which we will look at in this plan for additional context, address the mutual instructions given to Christians. But looking at the "one another" commands as a group gives us a powerful picture of the reciprocal relationship we should hope for, expect, and model with other believers.

How do we live out the "one another" commands?

These commands are not a means of earning salvation, but a way of living as people made new through the life, death, and resurrection of Jesus Christ. It is His resurrection that gives us the opportunity to walk in new life with Him, and it is the Holy Spirit that continues to transform us and equip us for lifelong obedience.

A New Command

"SEE ALSO" PASSAGES

Listed here are
additional passages with
"one another" commands
that are not included in
the day's reading.

SEE ALSO:
2 John 4–5

John 13:31–35

THE NEW COMMAND

[31] When he had left, Jesus said, "Now the Son of Man is glorified, and God is glorified in him. [32] If God is glorified in him, God will also glorify him in himself and will glorify him at once. [33] Little children, I am with you a little while longer. You will look for me, and just as I told the Jews, so now I tell you, 'Where I am going, you cannot come.'

PRIMARY READING

These main passages include "one another" commands related to the theme of today's reading.

[34] "I give you a new command: Love **one another**. Just as I have loved you, you are also to love **one another**. [35] By this everyone will know that you are my disciples, if you love **one another**."

John 15:1–17

THE VINE AND THE BRANCHES

[1] "I am the true vine, and my Father is the gardener. [2] Every branch in me that does not produce fruit he removes, and he prunes every branch that produces fruit so that it will

produce more fruit. [3] You are already clean because of the word I have spoken to you. [4] Remain in me, and I in you. Just as a branch is unable to produce fruit by itself unless it remains on the vine, neither can you unless you remain in me. [5] I am the vine; you are the branches. The one who remains in me and I in him produces much fruit, because you can do nothing without me. [6] If anyone does not remain in me, he is thrown aside like a branch and he withers. They gather them, throw them into the fire, and they are burned. [7] If you remain in me and my words remain in you, ask whatever you want and it will be done for you. [8] My Father is glorified by this: that you produce much fruit and prove to be my disciples.

CHRISTLIKE LOVE

[9] "As the Father has loved me, I have also loved you. Remain in my love. [10] If you keep my commands you will remain in my love, just as I have kept my Father's commands and remain in his love.

[11] "I have told you these things so that my joy may be in you and your joy may be complete.

[12] "This is my command: Love **one another** as I have loved you. [13] No one has greater love than this: to lay down his life for his friends. [14] You are my friends if you do what I command you. [15] I do not call you servants anymore, because a servant doesn't know what his master is doing. I have called you friends, because I have made known to you everything I have heard from my Father. [16] You did not choose me, but I chose you. I appointed you to go and produce fruit and that your fruit should remain, so that whatever you ask the Father in my name, he will give you.

[17] "This is what I command you: Love **one another**."

Romans 13:8-10

LOVE, OUR PRIMARY DUTY

ADDITIONAL READING

These passages show how today's theme is present throughout Scripture. Each additional passage is indicated by a taupe Scripture heading. ———

[8] Do not owe anyone anything, except to love **one another**, for the one who loves another has fulfilled the law. [9] The commandments, Do not commit adultery; do not murder; do not steal; do not covet; and any other commandment, are summed up by this commandment: Love your neighbor as yourself. [10] Love does no wrong to a neighbor. Love, therefore, is the fulfillment of the law.

Leviticus 19:18

"Do not take revenge or bear a grudge against members of your community, but love your neighbor as yourself; I am the Lord."

DAILY REFLECTION

Each weekday features
repeated questions to
help you connect with
what you are reading.

OBSERVE

REFLECT

RESPOND

How does the context
surrounding each "one another"
command in today's reading
provide clarity on life in
Christian community?

Write a prayer of confession or
gratitude reflecting on today's
reading. Ask for grace and growth
in living out these instructions.

How can you practically
live out the instructions from
today's reading in pursuing
fellowship with your brothers
and sisters in Christ?

Kingdom

The Upside-Down Kingdom

During His ministry on earth, Jesus often showed the radical difference between His kingdom and the one of this world, illustrating what life in the Spirit looks like for believers. It is a life where suffering leads to glory, weakness leads to strength, and letting go of the world means inheriting the earth. The "upside-down" nature of Christ's kingdom also reframes our understanding of the human experience, including how we relate to the world and one another.

Here are some other examples of the upside-down nature of the kingdom that Jesus established during His ministry on earth.

"Blessed are the poor in spirit,
for the kingdom of heaven is theirs."

Mt 5:3

"Blessed are those who mourn,
for they will be comforted."

Mt 5:4

"Blessed are those who hunger and
thirst for righteousness, for they will
be filled."

Mt 5:6

"Blessed are those who are persecuted
because of righteousness, for the
kingdom of heaven is theirs."

Mt 5:10

"But I tell you, don't resist an evildoer.
On the contrary, if anyone slaps you
on your right cheek, turn the other to
him also."

Mt 5:39

"You have heard that it was said, Love
your neighbor and hate your enemy.
But I tell you, love your enemies and
pray for those who persecute you…"

Mt 5:43–44

"Anyone who finds his life will lose it,
and anyone who loses his life because
of me will find it."

Mt 10:39

"So the last will be first, and the first last."

Mt 20:16

"Whoever wants to become great among
you must be your servant, and whoever wants
to be first among you must be your slave…"

Mt 20:26–27

Remember the words of the Lord Jesus,
because he said, "It is more blessed to give
than to receive."

Ac 20:35

Though he was rich, for your sake he
became poor, so that by his poverty you
might become rich.

2Co 8:9

…who, existing in the form of God, did not
consider equality with God as something to
be exploited. Instead he emptied himself by
assuming the form of a servant…for this
reason God highly exalted him.

Php 2:6–7, 9

Living Lives of Love

SEE ALSO:

1 Thessalonians 3:11–13; 4:9
2 Thessalonians 1:3

1 John 3:11–24

LOVE IN ACTION

[11] For this is the message you have heard from the beginning: We should love **one another**, [12] unlike Cain, who was of the evil one and murdered his brother. And why did he murder him? Because his deeds were evil, and his brother's were righteous.

[13] Do not be surprised, brothers and sisters, if the world hates you. [14] We know that we have passed from death to life because we love our brothers and sisters. The one who does not love remains in death. [15] Everyone who hates his brother or sister is a murderer, and you know that no murderer has eternal life residing in him. [16] This is how we have come to know love: He laid down his life for us. We should also lay down our lives for our brothers and sisters. [17] If anyone has this world's goods and sees a fellow believer in need but withholds compassion from him—how does God's love reside in him? [18] Little children, let us not love in word or speech, but in action and in truth.

[19] This is how we will know that we belong to the truth and will reassure our hearts before him [20] whenever our hearts condemn us; for God is greater than our hearts, and he knows all things.

[21] Dear friends, if our hearts don't condemn us, we have confidence before God [22] and receive whatever we ask from him because we keep his commands and do what is pleasing in his sight. [23] Now this is his command: that we believe in the name of his Son, Jesus Christ, and love **one another** as he commanded us. [24] The one who keeps his commands remains in him, and he in him. And the way we know that he remains in us is from the Spirit he has given us.

1 John 4:7–21

KNOWING GOD THROUGH LOVE

[7] Dear friends, let us love **one another**, because love is from God, and everyone who loves has been born of God and knows God. [8] The one who does not love does not know God, because God is love. [9] God's love was revealed among us in this way: God sent his one and only Son into the world so that we might live through him. [10] Love consists in this: not that we loved God, but that he loved us and sent his Son to be the atoning sacrifice for our sins. [11] Dear friends, if God loved us in this way, we also must love **one another**. [12] No one has ever seen God. If we love **one another**, God remains in us and his love is made complete in us. [13] This is how we know that we remain in him and he in us: He has given us of his Spirit. [14] And we have seen and we testify that the Father has sent his Son as the world's Savior. [15] Whoever confesses that Jesus is the Son of God—God remains in him and he in God. [16] And we have come to know and to believe the love that God has for us.

God is love, and the one who remains in love remains in God, and God remains in him. [17] In this, love is made complete with us so that we may have confidence in the day of judgment, because as he is, so also are we in this world. [18] There is no fear in love; instead, perfect love drives out fear, because fear involves punishment. So the one who fears is not complete in love. [19] We love because he first loved us. [20] If anyone says, "I love God," and yet hates his brother or sister, he is a liar. For the person who does not love his brother or sister whom he has seen cannot love God whom he has not seen. [21] And we have this command from him: The one who loves God must also love his brother and sister.

1 Peter 1:13–25

A CALL TO HOLY LIVING

[13] Therefore, with your minds ready for action, be sober-minded and set your hope completely on the grace to be brought to you at the revelation of Jesus Christ. [14] As obedient children, do not be conformed to the desires of your former ignorance. [15] But as the one who called you is holy, you also are to be holy in all your conduct; [16] for it is written, Be holy, because I am holy. [17] If you appeal to the Father who judges impartially according to each one's work, you are to conduct yourselves in reverence during your time living as strangers. [18] For you know that you were redeemed from your empty way of life inherited from your ancestors, not with perishable things like silver

---

Little children, let us not love in word or speech, but in action and in truth.

1 John 3:18

or gold, [19] but with the precious blood of Christ, like that of an unblemished and spotless lamb. [20] He was foreknown before the foundation of the world but was revealed in these last times for you. [21] Through him you believe in God, who raised him from the dead and gave him glory, so that your faith and hope are in God.

[22] Since you have purified yourselves by your obedience to the truth, so that you show sincere brotherly love for each other, from a pure heart love **one another** constantly, [23] because you have been born again—not of perishable seed but of imperishable—through the living and enduring word of God. [24] For

All flesh is like grass,
and all its glory like a flower of the grass.
The grass withers, and the flower falls,
[25] but the word of the Lord endures forever.

And this word is the gospel that was proclaimed to you.

Proverbs 3:3–4

[3] Never let loyalty and faithfulness leave you.
Tie them around your neck;
write them on the tablet of your heart.
[4] Then you will find favor and high regard
with God and people.

OBSERVE

REFLECT

RESPOND

How does the context surrounding each "one another" command in today's reading provide clarity on life in Christian community? How do today's instructions relate to the others we've read so far?

Write a prayer of confession or gratitude reflecting on today's reading. Ask for grace and growth in living out these instructions.

How can you practically live out the instructions from today's reading in pursuing fellowship with your brothers and sisters in Christ?

Considering Others

Philippians 2:1–11

CHRISTIAN HUMILITY

¹ If, then, there is any encouragement in Christ, if any consolation of love, if any fellowship with the Spirit, if any affection and mercy, ² make my joy complete by thinking the same way, having the same love, united in spirit, intent on one purpose. ³ Do nothing out of selfish ambition or conceit, but in humility consider others as more important than yourselves. ⁴ Everyone should look not to his own interests, but rather to the interests of others.

CHRIST'S HUMILITY AND EXALTATION

⁵ Adopt the same attitude as that of Christ Jesus,

⁶ who, existing in the form of God,
did not consider equality with God
as something to be exploited.
⁷ Instead he emptied himself

by assuming the form of a servant,
taking on the likeness of humanity.
And when he had come as a man,
⁸ he humbled himself by becoming obedient
to the point of death—
even to death on a cross.
⁹ For this reason God highly exalted him
and gave him the name
that is above every name,
¹⁰ so that at the name of Jesus
every knee will bow—
in heaven and on earth
and under the earth—
¹¹ and every tongue will confess
that Jesus Christ is Lord,
to the glory of God the Father.

John 13:1–7, 12–20

[1] Before the Passover Festival, Jesus knew that his hour had come to depart from this world to the Father. Having loved his own who were in the world, he loved them to the end.

[2] Now when it was time for supper, the devil had already put it into the heart of Judas, Simon Iscariot's son, to betray him. [3] Jesus knew that the Father had given everything into his hands, that he had come from God, and that he was going back to God. [4] So he got up from supper, laid aside his outer clothing, took a towel, and tied it around himself. [5] Next, he poured water into a basin and began to wash his disciples' feet and to dry them with the towel tied around him.

[6] He came to Simon Peter, who asked him, "Lord, are you going to wash my feet?"

[7] Jesus answered him, "What I'm doing you don't realize now, but afterward you will understand."

…

THE MEANING OF FOOT WASHING

[12] When Jesus had washed their feet and put on his outer clothing, he reclined again and said to them, "Do you know what I have done for you? [13] You call me Teacher and Lord—and you are speaking rightly, since that is what I am. [14] So if I, your Lord and Teacher, have washed your feet, you also ought to wash **one another's** feet. [15] For I have given you an example, that you also should do just as I have done for you.

[16] "Truly I tell you, a servant is not greater than his master, and a messenger is not greater than the one who sent him. [17] If you know these things, you are blessed if you do them.

[18] "I'm not speaking about all of you; I know those I have chosen. But the Scripture must be fulfilled: The one who eats my bread has raised his heel against me. [19] I am telling you now before it happens, so that when it does happen you will believe that I am he. [20] Truly I tell you, whoever receives anyone I send receives me, and the one who receives me receives him who sent me."

Romans 12:9–21

[9] Let love be without hypocrisy. Detest evil; cling to what is good. [10] Love **one another** deeply as brothers and sisters. Take the lead in honoring **one another**. [11] Do not lack diligence in zeal; be fervent in the Spirit; serve the Lord. [12] Rejoice in hope; be patient in affliction; be persistent in prayer. [13] Share with the saints in their needs; pursue hospitality. [14] Bless those who persecute you; bless and do not curse. [15] Rejoice with those who rejoice; weep with those who weep. [16] Live in harmony with **one another**. Do not be proud; instead, associate with the humble. Do not be wise in your own estimation. [17] Do not repay anyone evil for evil. Give careful thought to do what is honorable in everyone's eyes. [18] If possible, as far as it depends on you, live at peace with everyone. [19] Friends, do not avenge yourselves; instead, leave room for God's wrath, because it is written, Vengeance belongs to me; I will repay, says the Lord. [20] But

> If your enemy is hungry, feed him.
> If he is thirsty, give him something to drink.
> For in so doing
> you will be heaping fiery coals on his head.

[21] Do not be conquered by evil, but conquer evil with good.

Isaiah 66:2

> "My hand made all these things,
> and so they all came into being.
>   This is the Lord's declaration.
> I will look favorably on this kind of person:
> one who is humble, submissive in spirit,
> and trembles at my word."

OBSERVE

How does the context surrounding each "one another" command in today's reading provide clarity on life in Christian community? How do today's instructions relate to the others we've read so far?

REFLECT

Write a prayer of confession or gratitude reflecting on today's reading. Ask for grace and growth in living out these instructions.

RESPOND

How can you practically live out the instructions from today's reading in pursuing fellowship with your brothers and sisters in Christ?

Pursuing Unity

1 John 1:5–10

FELLOWSHIP WITH GOD

[5] This is the message we have heard from him and declare to you: God is light, and there is absolutely no darkness in him. [6] If we say, "We have fellowship with him," and yet we walk in darkness, we are lying and are not practicing the truth. [7] If we walk in the light as he himself is in the light, we have fellowship with **one another**, and the blood of Jesus his Son cleanses us from all sin. [8] If we say, "We have no sin," we are deceiving ourselves, and the truth is not in us. [9] If we confess our sins, he is faithful and righteous to forgive us our sins and to cleanse us from all unrighteousness. [10] If we say, "We have not sinned," we make him a liar, and his word is not in us.

Galatians 5:16–26

THE SPIRIT VERSUS THE FLESH

[16] I say, then, walk by the Spirit and you will certainly not carry out the desire of the flesh. [17] For the flesh desires what is against the Spirit, and the Spirit desires what is against the flesh; these are opposed to each other, so that you don't do what you want. [18] But if you are led by the Spirit, you are not under the law.

[19] Now the works of the flesh are obvious: sexual immorality, moral impurity, promiscuity, [20] idolatry, sorcery, hatreds, strife, jealousy, outbursts of anger, selfish ambitions, dissensions, factions, [21] envy, drunkenness, carousing, and anything similar. I am warning you about these things—as I warned you before—that those who practice such things will not inherit the kingdom of God.

[22] But the fruit of the Spirit is love, joy, peace, patience, kindness, goodness, faithfulness, [23] gentleness, and self-control. The law is not against such things. [24] Now those who belong to Christ Jesus have crucified the flesh with its passions and desires. [25] If we live by the Spirit, let us also keep in step with the Spirit. [26] Let us not become conceited, provoking **one another**, envying **one another**.

Romans 12:3-8

MANY GIFTS BUT ONE BODY

³ For by the grace given to me, I tell everyone among you not to think of himself more highly than he should think. Instead, think sensibly, as God has distributed a measure of faith to each one. ⁴ Now as we have many parts in one body, and all the parts do not have the same function, ⁵ in the same way we who are many are one body in Christ and individually members of **one another**. ⁶ According to the grace given to us, we have different gifts: If prophecy, use it according to the proportion of one's faith; ⁷ if service, use it in service; if teaching, in teaching; ⁸ if exhorting, in exhortation; giving, with generosity; leading, with diligence; showing mercy, with cheerfulness.

1 Corinthians 12:4-27

⁴ Now there are different gifts, but the same Spirit. ⁵ There are different ministries, but the same Lord. ⁶ And there are different activities, but the same God works all of them in each person. ⁷ A manifestation of the Spirit is given to each person for the common good: ⁸ to one is given a message of wisdom through the Spirit, to another, a message of knowledge by the same Spirit, ⁹ to another, faith by the same Spirit, to another, gifts of healing by the one Spirit, ¹⁰ to another, the performing of miracles, to another, prophecy, to another, distinguishing between spirits, to another, different kinds of tongues, to another, interpretation of tongues. ¹¹ One and the same Spirit is active in all these, distributing to each person as he wills.

UNITY YET DIVERSITY IN THE BODY

¹² For just as the body is one and has many parts, and all the parts of that body, though many, are one body—so also is Christ. ¹³ For we were all baptized by one Spirit into one body—whether Jews or Greeks, whether slaves or free—and we were all given one Spirit to drink. ¹⁴ Indeed, the body is not one part but many. ¹⁵ If the foot should say, "Because I'm not a hand, I don't belong to the body," it is not for that reason any less a part of the body. ¹⁶ And if the ear should say, "Because I'm not an eye, I don't belong to the body," it is not for that reason any less a part of the body. ¹⁷ If the whole body were an eye, where would the hearing be? If the whole body were an ear, where would the sense of smell be? ¹⁸ But as it is, God has arranged each one of the parts in the body just as he wanted. ¹⁹ And if they were all the same part, where would the body be? ²⁰ As it is, there are many parts, but one body. ²¹ The eye cannot say to the hand, "I don't need you!" Or again, the head can't say to the feet, "I don't need you!" ²² On the

In the same way we who are many are one body in Christ.

Romans 12:5

A manifestation of the Spirit is given to each person for the common good.

1 Corinthians 12:7

———

contrary, those parts of the body that are weaker are indispensable. [23] And those parts of the body that we consider less honorable, we clothe these with greater honor, and our unrespectable parts are treated with greater respect, [24] which our respectable parts do not need.

Instead, God has put the body together, giving greater honor to the less honorable, [25] so that there would be no division in the body, but that the members would have the same concern for each other. [26] So if one member suffers, all the members suffer with it; if one member is honored, all the members rejoice with it.

[27] Now you are the body of Christ, and individual members of it.

Psalm 133:1

How delightfully good
when brothers live together in harmony!

OBSERVE

How does the context
surrounding each "one another"
command in today's reading
provide clarity on life in
Christian community? How do
today's instructions relate to the
others we've read so far?

REFLECT

Write a prayer of confession or
gratitude reflecting on today's
reading. Ask for grace and growth
in living out these instructions.

RESPOND

How can you practically
live out the instructions from
today's reading in pursuing
fellowship with your brothers
and sisters in Christ?

Carrying Burdens

Galatians 6:1-10

CARRY ONE ANOTHER'S BURDENS

[1] Brothers and sisters, if someone is overtaken in any wrongdoing, you who are spiritual, restore such a person with a gentle spirit, watching out for yourselves so that you also won't be tempted. [2] Carry **one another's** burdens; in this way you will fulfill the law of Christ. [3] For if anyone considers himself to be something when he is nothing, he deceives himself. [4] Let each person examine his own work, and then he can take pride in himself alone, and not compare himself with someone else. [5] For each person will have to carry his own load.

[6] Let the one who is taught the word share all his good things with the teacher. [7] Don't be deceived: God is not mocked. For whatever a person sows he will also reap, [8] because the one who sows to his flesh will reap destruction from the flesh, but the one who sows to the Spirit will reap eternal life from the Spirit. [9] Let us not get tired of doing good, for we will reap at the proper time if we don't give up. [10] Therefore, as we have opportunity, let us work for the good of all, especially for those who belong to the household of faith.

Romans 14:13-23

THE LAW OF LOVE

[13] Therefore, let us no longer judge **one another**. Instead decide never to put a stumbling block or pitfall in the way of your brother or sister. [14] I know and am persuaded in the Lord Jesus that nothing is unclean in itself. Still, to someone who considers a thing to be unclean, to that one it is unclean. [15] For if your brother or sister is hurt by what you eat, you are no longer walking according to love. Do not destroy, by what you eat, someone for whom Christ died. [16] Therefore, do not let your good be slandered, [17] for the kingdom of God is not eating and drinking, but righteousness, peace, and joy in the Holy Spirit. [18] Whoever serves Christ in this way is acceptable to God and receives human approval.

[19] So then, let us pursue what promotes peace and what builds up **one another**. [20] Do not tear down God's work because of food. Everything is clean, but it is wrong to make someone fall by what he eats. [21] It is a good thing not to eat meat, or drink wine, or do anything that makes your brother or sister stumble. [22] Whatever you believe about these things, keep between yourself and God. Blessed is the one who

does not condemn himself by what he approves. [23] But whoever doubts stands condemned if he eats, because his eating is not from faith, and everything that is not from faith is sin.

James 5:13–20

EFFECTIVE PRAYER

[13] Is anyone among you suffering? He should pray. Is anyone cheerful? He should sing praises. [14] Is anyone among you sick? He should call for the elders of the church, and they are to pray over him, anointing him with oil in the name of the Lord. [15] The prayer of faith will save the sick person, and the Lord will raise him up; if he has committed sins, he will be forgiven. [16] Therefore, confess your sins to **one another** and pray for **one another**, so that you may be healed. The prayer of a righteous person is very powerful in its effect. [17] Elijah was a human being as we are, and he prayed earnestly that it would not rain, and for three years and six months it did not rain on the land. [18] Then he prayed again, and the sky gave rain and the land produced its fruit.

[19] My brothers and sisters, if any among you strays from the truth, and someone turns him back, [20] let that person know that whoever turns a sinner from the error of his way will save his soul from death and cover a multitude of sins.

Exodus 17:9–13

[9] Moses said to Joshua, "Select some men for us and go fight against Amalek. Tomorrow I will stand on the hilltop with God's staff in my hand."

[10] Joshua did as Moses had told him, and fought against Amalek, while Moses, Aaron, and Hur went up to the top of the hill. [11] While Moses held up his hand, Israel prevailed, but whenever he put his hand down, Amalek prevailed. [12] When Moses's hands grew heavy, they took a stone and put it under him, and he sat down on it. Then Aaron and Hur supported his hands, one on one side and one on the other so that his hands remained steady until the sun went down. [13] So Joshua defeated Amalek and his army with the sword.

OBSERVE

How does the context
surrounding each "one another"
command in today's reading
provide clarity on life in
Christian community? How do
today's instructions relate to the
others we've read so far?

REFLECT

Write a prayer of confession or
gratitude reflecting on today's
reading. Ask for grace and growth
in living out these instructions.

RESPOND

How can you practically
live out the instructions from
today's reading in pursuing
fellowship with your brothers
and sisters in Christ?

Take this day to catch up on your reading, pray, and rest in the presence of the Lord.

Never let loyalty and faithfulness leave you. Tie them around your neck; write them on the tablet of your heart. Then you will find favor and high regard with God and people.

PROVERBS 3:3–4

Weekly Truth

DAY 07

Scripture is God-breathed and true. When we memorize it, we carry the good news of Jesus with us wherever we go.

During this study, we will memorize the key passage for this reading plan, Romans 15:5–6. In this passage, the apostle Paul speaks a blessing over his readers that expresses his desire for their collective unity. Read the full blessing aloud a few times, then try saying it from memory.

Now may the God who gives endurance and encouragement grant you to live in harmony with one another, according to Christ Jesus, so that you may glorify the God and Father of our Lord Jesus Christ with one mind and one voice.

ROMANS 15:5–6

Offering Hospitality

Romans 15:1–13

PLEASING OTHERS, NOT OURSELVES

[1] Now we who are strong have an obligation to bear the weaknesses of those without strength, and not to please ourselves. [2] Each one of us is to please his neighbor for his good, to build him up. [3] For even Christ did not please himself. On the contrary, as it is written, The insults of those who insult you have fallen on me. [4] For whatever was written in the past was written for our instruction, so that we may have hope through endurance and through the encouragement from the Scriptures. [5] Now may the God who gives endurance and encouragement grant you to live in harmony with **one another**, according to Christ Jesus, [6] so that you may glorify the God and Father of our Lord Jesus Christ with one mind and one voice.

GLORIFYING GOD TOGETHER

[7] Therefore welcome **one another**, just as Christ also welcomed you, to the glory of God. [8] For I say that Christ became a servant of the circumcised on behalf of God's truth, to confirm the promises to the fathers, [9] and so that Gentiles may glorify God for his mercy. As it is written,

> Therefore I will praise you among the Gentiles,
> and I will sing praise to your name.

[10] Again it says, Rejoice, you Gentiles, with his people! [11] And again,

> Praise the Lord, all you Gentiles;
> let all the peoples praise him!

[12] And again, Isaiah says,

> The root of Jesse will appear,
> the one who rises to rule the Gentiles;
> the Gentiles will hope in him.

[13] Now may the God of hope fill you with all joy and peace as you believe so that you may overflow with hope by the power of the Holy Spirit.

1 Corinthians 11:27–34

SELF-EXAMINATION

[27] So, then, whoever eats the bread or drinks the cup of the Lord in an unworthy manner will be guilty of sin against the body and blood of the Lord. [28] Let a person examine himself; in this way let him eat the bread and drink from the cup. [29] For whoever eats and drinks without recognizing the body, eats and drinks judgment on himself. [30] This is why many are sick and ill among you, and many have fallen asleep. [31] If we were properly judging ourselves, we would not be judged, [32] but when we are judged by the Lord, we are disciplined, so that we may not be condemned with the world.

[33] Therefore, my brothers and sisters, when you come together to eat, welcome **one another**. [34] If anyone is hungry, he should eat at home, so that when you gather together you will not come under judgment. I will give instructions about the other matters whenever I come.

1 Peter 4:7–11 NIV

[7] The end of all things is near. Therefore be alert and of sober mind so that you may pray. [8] Above all, love each other deeply, because love covers over a multitude of sins. [9] Offer hospitality to **one another** without grumbling. [10] Each of you should use whatever gift you have received to serve others, as faithful stewards of God's grace in its various forms. [11] If anyone speaks, they should do so as one who speaks the very words of God. If anyone serves, they should do so with the strength God provides, so that in all things God may be praised through Jesus Christ. To him be the glory and the power for ever and ever. Amen.

Proverbs 21:10

A wicked person desires evil;
he has no consideration for his neighbor.

OBSERVE

How does the context surrounding each "one another" command in today's reading provide clarity on life in Christian community? How do today's instructions relate to the others we've read so far?

REFLECT

Write a prayer of confession or gratitude reflecting on today's reading. Ask for grace and growth in living out these instructions.

RESPOND

How can you practically live out the instructions from today's reading in pursuing fellowship with your brothers and sisters in Christ?

Submitting to Authority

Ephesians 5:15–21

CONSISTENCY IN THE CHRISTIAN LIFE

[15] Pay careful attention, then, to how you walk—not as unwise people but as wise— [16] making the most of the time, because the days are evil. [17] So don't be foolish, but understand what the Lord's will is. [18] And don't get drunk with wine, which leads to reckless living, but be filled by the Spirit: [19] speaking to one another in psalms, hymns, and spiritual songs, singing and making music with your heart to the Lord, [20] giving thanks always for everything to God the Father in the name of our Lord Jesus Christ, [21] submitting to **one another** in the fear of Christ.

1 Peter 5:1–9

ABOUT THE ELDERS

[1] I exhort the elders among you as a fellow elder and witness to the sufferings of Christ, as well as one who shares in the glory about to be revealed: [2] Shepherd God's flock among you, not overseeing out of compulsion but willingly, as God would have you; not out of greed for money but eagerly; [3] not lording it over those entrusted to you, but being examples to the flock. [4] And when the chief Shepherd appears, you will receive the unfading crown of glory. [5] In the same way, you who are younger, be subject to the elders. All of you clothe yourselves with humility toward **one another**, because

God resists the proud
but gives grace to the humble.

CONCLUSION

[6] Humble yourselves, therefore, under the mighty hand of God, so that he may exalt you at the proper time, [7] casting all your cares on him, because he cares about you. [8] Be sober-minded, be alert. Your adversary the devil is prowling around like a roaring lion, looking for anyone he can devour.

⁹ Resist him, firm in the faith, knowing that the same kind of sufferings are being experienced by your fellow believers throughout the world.

Jeremiah 23:3–4

³ "I will gather the remnant of my flock from all the lands where I have banished them, and I will return them to their grazing land. They will become fruitful and numerous. ⁴ I will raise up shepherds over them who will tend them. They will no longer be afraid or discouraged, nor will any be missing." This is the LORD's declaration.

Daniel 2:21

He changes the times and seasons;
he removes kings and establishes kings.
He gives wisdom to the wise
and knowledge to those
who have understanding.

Proverbs 27:6, 9, 17–18

⁶ The wounds of a friend are trustworthy,
but the kisses of an enemy are excessive.

…

⁹ Oil and incense bring joy to the heart,
and the sweetness of a friend is better than self-counsel.

…

¹⁷ Iron sharpens iron,
and one person sharpens another.

¹⁸ Whoever tends a fig tree will eat its fruit,
and whoever looks after his master will be honored.

OBSERVE

REFLECT

RESPOND

How does the context surrounding each "one another" command in today's reading provide clarity on life in Christian community? How do today's instructions relate to the others we've read so far?

Write a prayer of confession or gratitude reflecting on today's reading. Ask for grace and growth in living out these instructions.

How can you practically live out the instructions from today's reading in pursuing fellowship with your brothers and sisters in Christ?

Avoiding Division

James 4:1–12

PROUD OR HUMBLE

[1] What is the source of wars and fights among you? Don't they come from your passions that wage war within you? [2] You desire and do not have. You murder and covet and cannot obtain. You fight and wage war. You do not have because you do not ask. [3] You ask and don't receive because you ask with wrong motives, so that you may spend it on your pleasures.

[4] You adulterous people! Don't you know that friendship with the world is hostility toward God? So whoever wants to be the friend of the world becomes the enemy of God. [5] Or do you think it's without reason that the Scripture says: The spirit he made to dwell in us envies intensely?

[6] But he gives greater grace. Therefore he says:

> God resists the proud
> but gives grace to the humble.

[7] Therefore, submit to God. Resist the devil, and he will flee from you. [8] Draw near to God, and he will draw near to you. Cleanse your hands, sinners, and purify your hearts, you double-minded. [9] Be miserable and mourn and weep.

Let your laughter be turned to mourning and your joy to gloom. [10] Humble yourselves before the Lord, and he will exalt you.

[11] Don't criticize **one another**, brothers and sisters. Anyone who defames or judges a fellow believer defames and judges the law. If you judge the law, you are not a doer of the law but a judge. [12] There is one lawgiver and judge who is able to save and to destroy. But who are you to judge your neighbor?

James 5:7–11

WAITING FOR THE LORD

[7] Therefore, brothers and sisters, be patient until the Lord's coming. See how the farmer waits for the precious fruit of the earth and is patient with it until it receives the early and the late rains. [8] You also must be patient. Strengthen your hearts, because the Lord's coming is near.

[9] Brothers and sisters, do not complain about **one another**, so that you will not be judged. Look, the judge stands at the door!

[10] Brothers and sisters, take the prophets who spoke in the Lord's name as an example of suffering and patience. [11] See, we count as blessed those who have endured. You have heard of Job's endurance and have seen the outcome that the Lord brought about—the Lord is compassionate and merciful.

Galatians 5:13–15

[13] For you were called to be free, brothers and sisters; only don't use this freedom as an opportunity for the flesh, but serve **one another** through love. [14] For the whole law is fulfilled in one statement: Love your neighbor as yourself. [15] But if you bite and devour **one another**, watch out, or you will be consumed by **one another**.

Mark 9:42–50

WARNINGS FROM JESUS

[42] "But whoever causes one of these little ones who believe in me to fall away —it would be better for him if a heavy millstone were hung around his neck and he were thrown into the sea.

Strengthen your hearts, because the Lord's coming is near.

James 5:8

Love your neighbor as yourself.

Galatians 5:14

———

43 "And if your hand causes you to fall away, cut it off. It is better for you to enter life maimed than to have two hands and go to hell, the unquenchable fire. 45 And if your foot causes you to fall away, cut it off. It is better for you to enter life lame than to have two feet and be thrown into hell. 47 And if your eye causes you to fall away, gouge it out. It is better for you to enter the kingdom of God with one eye than to have two eyes and be thrown into hell, 48 where their worm does not die, and the fire is not quenched. 49 For everyone will be salted with fire. 50 Salt is good, but if the salt should lose its flavor, how can you season it? Have salt among yourselves, and be at peace with **one another**."

Zechariah 7:9–10

9 "The Lord of Armies says this: 'Make fair decisions. Show faithful love and compassion to one another. 10 Do not oppress the widow or the fatherless, the resident alien or the poor, and do not plot evil in your hearts against one another.'"

OBSERVE

How does the context surrounding each "one another" command in today's reading provide clarity on life in Christian community? How do today's instructions relate to the others we've read so far?

REFLECT

Write a prayer of confession or gratitude reflecting on today's reading. Ask for grace and growth in living out these instructions.

RESPOND

How can you practically live out the instructions from today's reading in pursuing fellowship with your brothers and sisters in Christ?

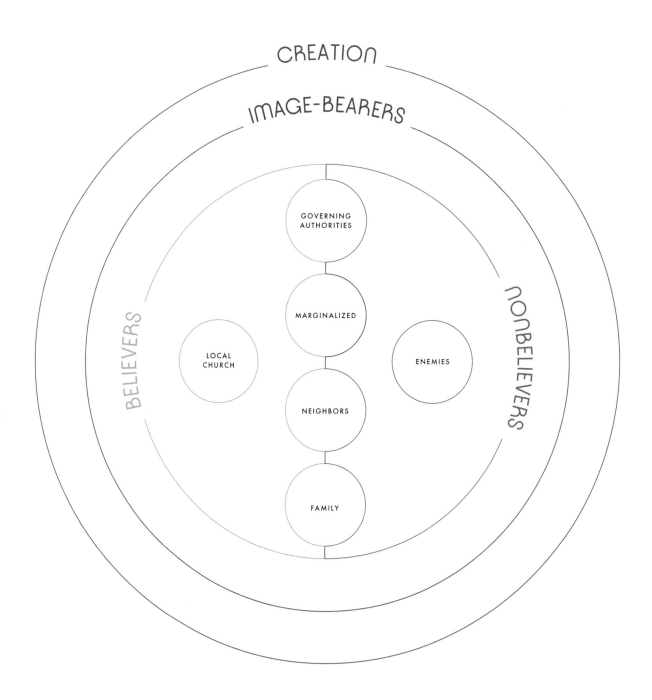

How Should I Relate To…?

The "one another" commands found in Scripture pay particular attention to believers' relationships with each other. But our new selves in Christ are called to think differently about every aspect of the world, from creation to the family unit to the local church and beyond. The following pages contain an overview of what Scripture says about the different ways Christians are called to interact with all God has made. The diagram on the opposite page depicts how these relationships build upon each other.

CREATION

Of all His created beings, God has given humans a unique role as caretakers of the earth. As His image-bearers we share in this responsibility of stewardship, or caring for all of God's creation. We are called to tend to creation until all things are fully renewed when Jesus returns.

Gn 1; 2:15
Ex 23:10–11
Lv 25:1–28
Rv 11:18

IMAGE-BEARERS

Every human being, regardless of age, race, economic class, and physical or mental ability, is made in the image of God. We have a responsibility to relate to all people, whether believers or nonbelievers, as those who bear this same image and are worthy of dignity and respect.

Gn 1:26–28; 5:1–2; 9:1–5
Jms 3:9–10

NONBELIEVERS

Followers of Jesus are not called to live apart from those who don't know Christ. Rather, we are to demonstrate Christ's love in how we live and to share the good news of His life, death, and resurrection with others. Scripture also instructs us to use discernment in these relationships, remaining aware of the influence those who don't know Jesus can have in our lives.

Mt 9:10–13; 28:19–20
Jn 4:1–26
2Co 6:14–17
Col 4:5–6

OTHER BELIEVERS

Christians are connected to one another in Christ. We are called to live out our relationships with one another as a demonstration of the unity and love made possible in Jesus.

See your daily reading for what Scripture says about these relationships.

LOCAL CHURCH

In addition to being part of the larger body of Christ around the world and across time, we are also called to be committed to a local group of believers. In this context, we hold one another accountable through discipleship and discipline.

Mt 18:15–20
Ac 2:42–47
Rm 12:3–8
Jms 5:13–18

ENEMIES

Throughout life we will encounter those who oppose God, His plan, and His people. We are instructed to refrain from retaliating or seeking revenge against those who mistreat us or seek our harm. Instead, we are called to "love our enemies" and "turn the other cheek," trusting that God will protect us from evil.

Dt 31:6
Pr 24:1–20
Mt 5:38–40, 43–48
Rm 12:17–21
1Pt 2:21–25; 3:9

GOVERNING AUTHORITIES

In almost every case, Christians are called to very simple instructions regarding governing authorities: obey and pray for those God has placed in authority. However, civil disobedience is permitted and required when a believer would have to disobey God in order to obey governing authorities. As those who are in relationship with a good and just God, Christians are also called to speak out against injustice.

Pr 31:8–9
Jr 22:1–5
Dn 3; 6:1–10
Am 5:4–15
Mk 12:17
Ac 5:25–32
Rm 13:1–2
1 Tm 2:1–2
1 Pt 2:13–14

MARGINALIZED

Throughout the Old Testament, God gave instructions on the just and merciful treatment of those belonging to the most disempowered groups in society—the widow, the fatherless, the foreigner, the enslaved, and those without rights or who were oppressed. In the New Testament, Jesus ministered to these marginalized people across different categories, whether foreigners, disenfranchised social groups, or those suffering from illness or physical limitation. As followers of Christ, we are called to follow this example, showing special care and protection for the most vulnerable members of society.

Dt 10:19; 15:12–18
Is 1:17
Mt 25:31–40
Lk 5:12–16; 9:46–48
Jms 2:1–13

NEIGHBORS

Jesus summed up the entirety of the Law in two commandments—love God and love our neighbors. We are to minister to our neighbors' needs, extending them the care we would show ourselves in any given situation.

Lv 19:18
Pr 3:29
Lk 10:25–37
Rm 13:9–10

FAMILY

Familial relationships echo the relationship believers share with God: the institution of marriage reflects the relationship between Christ and the Church, and parent-child relationships reflect the relationship between God the Father and His children. As part of representing God's kingdom, we are called to live out family relationships with mutual honor, love, and sacrifice, while resisting the temptation to idolize these relationships over our commitment to Jesus. At the same time, Jesus challenges us to expand our understanding of family, extending the boundaries beyond the nuclear unit to include other believers as our family in Christ.

Ex 20:12
Mk 3:31–35
Lk 14:25–26
Jn 19:25–27
Eph 5:22–33; 6:1–4
Col 3:22–25

Extending Forgiveness and Encouragement

SEE ALSO:

1 Corinthians 7:1–9
1 Thessalonians 4:13–18

Hebrews 10:1–25

THE PERFECT SACRIFICE

[1] Since the law has only a shadow of the good things to come, and not the reality itself of those things, it can never perfect the worshipers by the same sacrifices they continually offer year after year. [2] Otherwise, wouldn't they have stopped being offered, since the worshipers, purified once and for all, would no longer have any consciousness of sins? [3] But in the sacrifices there is a reminder of sins year after year. [4] For it is impossible for the blood of bulls and goats to take away sins.

[5] Therefore, as he was coming into the world, he said:

You did not desire sacrifice and offering,
but you prepared a body for me.
[6] You did not delight
in whole burnt offerings and sin offerings.
[7] Then I said, "See—
it is written about me
in the scroll—
I have come to do your will, God."

[8] After he says above, You did not desire or delight in sacrifices and offerings, whole burnt offerings and sin offerings (which are offered according to the law), [9] he then says, See, I have come to do your will. He takes away the first to establish the second. [10] By this will, we have been sanctified through the offering of the body of Jesus Christ once for all time.

[11] Every priest stands day after day ministering and offering the same sacrifices time after time, which can never take away sins. [12] But this man, after offering one sacrifice for sins forever, sat down at the right hand of God. [13] He is now waiting until his enemies are made his footstool. [14] For by one offering he has perfected forever those who are sanctified. [15] The Holy Spirit also testifies to us about this. For after he says:

[16] This is the covenant I will make with them after those days,

the Lord says,

I will put my laws on their hearts
and write them on their minds,

[17] and I will never again remember

their sins and their lawless acts.

[18] Now where there is forgiveness of these, there is no longer an offering for sin.

[19] Therefore, brothers and sisters, since we have boldness to enter the sanctuary through the blood of Jesus— [20] he has inaugurated for us a new and living way through the curtain (that is, through his flesh)— [21] and since we have a great high priest over the house of God, [22] let us draw near with a true heart in full assurance of faith, with our hearts sprinkled clean from an evil conscience and our bodies washed in pure water. [23] Let us hold on to the confession of our hope without wavering, since he who promised is faithful. [24] And let us consider **one another** in order to provoke love and good works, [25] not neglecting to gather together, as some are in the habit of doing, but encouraging each other, and all the more as you see the day approaching.

1 Thessalonians 5:1–24

THE DAY OF THE LORD

[1] About the times and the seasons: Brothers and sisters, you do not need anything to be written to you. [2] For you yourselves know very well that the day of the Lord will come just like a thief in the night. [3] When they say, "Peace and security," then sudden destruction will come upon them, like labor pains on a pregnant woman, and they will not escape. [4] But you, brothers and sisters, are not in the dark, for this day to surprise you like a thief. [5] For you are all children of light and children of the day. We do not belong to the night or the darkness. [6] So then, let us not sleep, like the rest, but let us stay awake and be self-controlled. [7] For those who sleep, sleep at night, and those who get drunk, get drunk at night. [8] But since we belong to the day, let us be self-controlled and put on the armor of faith and love, and a helmet of the hope of salvation. [9] For God did not appoint us to wrath, but to obtain salvation through our Lord Jesus Christ, [10] who died for us, so that whether we are awake or asleep, we may live together with him. [11] Therefore encourage **one another** and build each other up as you are already doing.

EXHORTATIONS AND BLESSINGS

[12] Now we ask you, brothers and sisters, to give recognition to those who labor among you and lead you in the Lord and admonish you, [13] and to regard them very highly in love because of their work. Be at peace among yourselves. [14] And we exhort you, brothers and sisters: warn those who are idle, comfort the discouraged, help the weak, be patient with everyone. [15] See to it that no one repays evil for evil to anyone, but always pursue what is good for **one another** and for all. [16] Rejoice always, [17] pray constantly, [18] give thanks in everything; for this is God's will for you in Christ Jesus. [19] Don't stifle the Spirit. [20] Don't despise prophecies, [21] but test all things. Hold on to what is good. [22] Stay away from every kind of evil.

[23] Now may the God of peace himself sanctify you completely. And may your whole spirit, soul, and body be kept sound and blameless at the coming of our Lord Jesus Christ. [24] He who calls you is faithful; he will do it.

Malachi 2:10

Don't all of us have one Father? Didn't one God create us? Why then do we act treacherously against one another, profaning the covenant of our ancestors?

OBSERVE

How does the context surrounding each "one another" command in today's reading provide clarity on life in Christian community? How do today's instructions relate to the others we've read so far?

REFLECT

Write a prayer of confession or gratitude reflecting on today's reading. Ask for grace and growth in living out these instructions.

RESPOND

How can you practically live out the instructions from today's reading in pursuing fellowship with your brothers and sisters in Christ?

Living in Community

Colossians 3:1–17

THE LIFE OF THE NEW MAN

[1] So if you have been raised with Christ, seek the things above, where Christ is, seated at the right hand of God. [2] Set your minds on things above, not on earthly things. [3] For you died, and your life is hidden with Christ in God. [4] When Christ, who is your life, appears, then you also will appear with him in glory.

[5] Therefore, put to death what belongs to your earthly nature: sexual immorality, impurity, lust, evil desire, and greed, which is idolatry. [6] Because of these, God's wrath is coming upon the disobedient, [7] and you once walked in these things when you were living in them. [8] But now, put away all the following: anger, wrath, malice, slander, and filthy language from your mouth. [9] Do not lie to **one another**, since you have put off the old self with its practices [10] and have put on the new self. You are being renewed in knowledge according to the image of your Creator. [11] In Christ there is not Greek and Jew, circumcision and uncircumcision, barbarian, Scythian, slave and free; but Christ is all and in all.

THE CHRISTIAN LIFE

[12] Therefore, as God's chosen ones, holy and dearly loved, put on compassion, kindness, humility, gentleness, and patience, [13] bearing with **one another** and forgiving **one another** if anyone has a grievance against another. Just as the Lord has forgiven you, so you are also to forgive. [14] Above all, put on love, which is the perfect bond of unity. [15] And let the peace of Christ, to which you were also called in one body, rule your hearts. And be thankful. [16] Let the word of Christ dwell richly among you, in all wisdom teaching and admonishing one another through psalms, hymns, and spiritual songs, singing to God with gratitude in your hearts. [17] And whatever you do, in word or in deed, do everything in the name of the Lord Jesus, giving thanks to God the Father through him.

Ephesians 4:17–32

LIVING THE NEW LIFE

[17] Therefore, I say this and testify in the Lord: You should no longer walk as the Gentiles do, in the futility of their thoughts. [18] They are darkened in their understanding, excluded from the life of God, because of the ignorance that is in them and because of the hardness of their hearts. [19] They became callous and gave themselves over to promiscuity for the practice of every kind of impurity with a desire for more and more.

[20] But that is not how you came to know Christ, [21] assuming you heard about him and were taught by him, as the truth is in Jesus, [22] to take off your former way of life, the old self that is corrupted by deceitful desires, [23] to be renewed in the spirit of your minds, [24] and to put on the new self, the one created according to God's likeness in righteousness and purity of the truth.

[25] Therefore, putting away lying, speak the truth, each one to his neighbor, because we are members of **one another**. [26] Be angry and do not sin. Don't let the sun go down on your anger, [27] and don't give the devil an opportunity. [28] Let the thief no longer steal. Instead, he is to do honest work with his own hands, so that he has something to share with anyone in need. [29] No foul language should come from your mouth, but only what is good for building up someone in need, so that it gives grace to those who hear. [30] And don't grieve God's Holy Spirit. You were sealed by him for the day of redemption. [31] Let all bitterness, anger and wrath, shouting and slander be removed from you, along with all malice. [32] And be kind and compassionate to **one another**, forgiving **one another**, just as God also forgave you in Christ.

Proverbs 11:17

A kind man benefits himself,
but a cruel person brings ruin on himself.

Zechariah 8:16–17

[16] "These are the things you must do: Speak truth to one another; make true and sound decisions within your city gates. [17] Do not plot evil in your hearts against your neighbor, and do not love perjury, for I hate all this"—this is the Lord's declaration.

OBSERVE

REFLECT

RESPOND

How does the context
surrounding each "one another"
command in today's reading
provide clarity on life in
Christian community? How do
today's instructions relate to the
others we've read so far?

Write a prayer of confession or
gratitude reflecting on today's
reading. Ask for grace and growth
in living out these instructions.

How can you practically
live out the instructions from
today's reading in pursuing
fellowship with your brothers
and sisters in Christ?

Grace Day

Take this day to catch up on your reading, pray,
and rest in the presence of the Lord.

"The LORD of Armies says this: 'Make fair decisions. Show faithful love and compassion to one another. Do not oppress the widow or the fatherless, the resident alien and poor, and do not plot evil in your hearts against one another.'"

ZECHARIAH 7:9–10

Weekly Truth

DAY 14

Scripture is God-breathed and true. When we memorize it, we carry the good news of Jesus with us wherever we go.

While studying the "one another" commands in the New Testament, we've memorized Romans 15:5–6. Write the passage three times in the space provided to help commit it to memory.

Now may the God who gives endurance and encouragement grant you to live in harmony with one another, according to Christ Jesus, so that you may glorify the God and Father of our Lord Jesus Christ with one mind and one voice.

ROMANS 15:5–6

Above all, put on love, which is the perfect bond of unity. And let the peace of Christ, to which you were also called in one body, rule your hearts. And be thankful. Let the word of

Christ dwell richly among you, in all wisdom teaching and admonishing one another through psalms, hymns, and spiritual songs, singing to God with gratitude in your hearts.

COLOSSIANS 3:14—16

CSB BOOK ABBREVIATIONS

BIBLIOGRAPHY

Kimble, J., et. al., eds. "Fellowship in the Life of the Church." In *Lexham Survey of Theology.* Bellingham: Lexham Press, 2018.

LOOKING FOR DEVOTIONALS?

Download the **She Reads Truth app** to find devotionals that complement your daily Scripture reading. If you're stuck on a passage, hop into the community discussion to instantly connect with other Shes who are reading God's Word right along with you. You can also highlight Bible passages and download free lock screens for Weekly Truth memorization—all on the She Reads Truth app.

 DOWNLOAD THE
SHE READS TRUTH
APP TODAY!

FOR THE RECORD

WHERE DID I STUDY?

O HOME
O OFFICE
O CHURCH
O SCHOOL
O COFFEE SHOP
O OTHER:

WHAT WAS I LISTENING TO?

ARTIST:

SONG:

PLAYLIST:

WHEN DID I STUDY?

O MORNING
O AFTERNOON
O NIGHT

HOW DID I FIND DELIGHT IN GOD'S WORD?

WHAT WAS HAPPENING IN MY LIFE?

WHAT WAS HAPPENING IN THE WORLD?

| MONTH | DAY | YEAR |

END DATE